Prepared in cooperation with the U.S. Fish and Wildlife Service

A Digital Model for Planning Water Management at Benton Lake National Wildlife Refuge, West-Central Montana

Scientific Investigations Report 2011–5133

U.S. Department of the Interior
U.S. Geological Survey

Cover. Snow geese over Benton Lake, Montana. Photograph by Mishler Photography, Neal and Mary Jane Mishler, taken March 21, 2007. Published with permission.

A Digital Model for Planning Water Management at Benton Lake National Wildlife Refuge, West-Central Montana

By David A. Nimick, Peter M. McCarthy, and Vanessa Fields

Prepared in cooperation with the U.S. Fish and Wildlife Service

Scientific Investigations Report 2011–5133

U.S. Department of the Interior
U.S. Geological Survey

U.S. Department of the Interior
KEN SALAZAR, Secretary

U.S. Geological Survey
Marcia K. McNutt, Director

U.S. Geological Survey, Reston, Virginia: 2011

For more information on the USGS—the Federal source for science about the Earth, its natural and living resources, natural hazards, and the environment, visit http://www.usgs.gov or call 1–888–ASK–USGS.

For an overview of USGS information products, including maps, imagery, and publications, visit http://www.usgs.gov/pubprod

To order this and other USGS information products, visit http://store.usgs.gov

Suggested citation:
Nimick, D.A., McCarthy, P.M., and Fields, Vanessa, 2011, A digital model for planning water management at Benton Lake National Wildlife Refuge, west-central Montana: U.S. Geological Survey Scientific Investigations Report 2011–5133, 28 p.

ISBN 78-1-4113-3218-8

Contents

Figures

Tables

Compact Disc

(In pocket at back of report. Files also available at *http://pubs.usgs.gov/sir/2011/5133*)

Format: American Standard Code for Information Interchange (ASCII) or Microsoft Excel 2007

Operating system used: Windows XP Professional

README.TXT

APPENDIX_2.xlsm—Digital Model for Planning Water Management at Benton Lake National Wildlife Refuge

Conversion Factors, Datum, and Abbreviations

Inch/Pound to SI

Multiply	By	To obtain
Length		
inch (in.)	2.54	centimeter (cm)
foot (ft)	0.3048	meter (m)
mile (mi)	1.609	kilometer (km)
Area		
acre	0.4047	hectare (ha)
square mile (mi^2)	259.0	hectare (ha)
Volume		
acre-foot (acre-ft)	1,233	cubic meter (m^3)
Flow rate		
acre-foot per day	0.01427	cubic meter per second (m^3/s)
cubic foot per second	0.02832	cubic meter per second (m^3/s)

Vertical coordinate information is referenced to the National Geodetic Vertical Datum of 1929 (NGVD 29).

Horizontal coordinate information is referenced to the North American Datum of 1927 (NAD 27).

Altitude, as used in this report, refers to distance above the vertical datum.

Abbreviations used in this report:

CD–ROM	compact disc–read-only memory
GUI	graphical user interface
NOAA	National Oceanic and Atmospheric Administration
NWR	National Wildlife Refuge
USFWS	U.S. Fish and Wildlife Service
USGS	U.S. Geological Survey
VBA	Visual Basic for Applications

A Digital Model for Planning Water Management at Benton Lake National Wildlife Refuge, West-Central Montana

By David A. Nimick[1], Peter M. McCarthy[1], and Vanessa Fields[2]

Abstract

Benton Lake National Wildlife Refuge is an important area for waterfowl production and migratory stopover in west-central Montana. Eight wetland units covering about 5,600 acres are the essential features of the refuge. Water availability for the wetland units can be uncertain owing to the large natural variations in precipitation and runoff and the high cost of pumping supplemental water. The U.S. Geological Survey, in cooperation with the U.S. Fish and Wildlife Service, has developed a digital model for planning water management. The model can simulate strategies for water transfers among the eight wetland units and account for variability in runoff and pumped water. This report describes this digital model, which uses a water-accounting spreadsheet to track inputs and outputs to each of the wetland units of Benton Lake National Wildlife Refuge. Inputs to the model include (1) monthly values for precipitation, pumped water, runoff, and evaporation; (2) water-level/capacity data for each wetland unit; and (3) the pan-evaporation coefficient. Outputs include monthly water volume and flooded surface area for each unit for as many as 5 consecutive years. The digital model was calibrated by comparing simulated and historical measured water volumes for specific test years.

Introduction

Benton Lake National Wildlife Refuge (NWR) is an important area for waterfowl production and migratory stopover in west-central Montana (fig. 1). Refuge managers are developing a comprehensive conservation plan to guide future refuge management. This plan will include an assessment of a range of management options, all of which depend to a large extent on water supply. The plan also may include assessments of major infrastructure projects, such as constructing a siphon to augment water supplied by transbasin diversion and rerouting the inflow of Lake Creek to mitigate selenium hazards in the wetland units that comprise Benton Lake. To better assess management options and determine how to make the best use of limited water, refuge managers need to be able to evaluate different water-management strategies. A digital model that can simulate water transfers among the wetland units and account for variability in runoff and pumped water would facilitate this evaluation. The U.S. Geological Survey (USGS), in cooperation with the U.S. Fish and Wildlife Service (USFWS), has developed such a digital model for Benton Lake NWR.

Purpose and Scope

The purpose of this report is to describe a digital model for planning water management for the wetlands at Benton Lake NWR. The model uses a water-accounting spreadsheet that tracks inputs and outputs to each of the wetland units of Benton Lake. User input to the model includes monthly values for precipitation, water pumped from Muddy Creek, and runoff, as well as the pan-evaporation coefficient. Input embedded in the model includes monthly values for evaporation and water-level/capacity data for each wetland unit. Model output includes monthly water volume and flooded surface area for each unit for as many as 5 consecutive years. The model was calibrated by comparing simulated and historical measured water volumes for specific test years. Instructions for the digital model are available in appendix 1, and the model is available on a compact disc–read-only memory (CD–ROM) in appendix 2 located in the inside back cover or at *http://pubs. usgs.gov/sir/2011/5133*.

Information and data used in this report were compiled from several sources. The general hydrology of Lake Creek and Benton Lake NWR has been described by Nimick and others (1996) and Nimick (1997). Precipitation data are available for three National Oceanic and Atmospheric Administration (NOAA) weather stations 11 to 14 miles (mi) from

---

[1]U.S. Geological Survey.

[2]U.S. Fish and Wildlife Service.

Benton Lake and for the station at the refuge headquarters. Streamflow in Lake Creek has been measured seasonally by the USGS (streamflow-gaging station 06090650) since 1991. Evaporation data are available for four NOAA weather stations 47 to 91 mi from Benton Lake and for the refuge headquarters. Historical data for estimated monthly amounts of pumped water and runoff as well as measured water levels in individual wetland units (fig. 1) are available in unpublished annual water-use reports available at the refuge headquarters (Benton Lake National Wildlife Refuge, issued annually).

Description of the Study Area

Benton Lake basin is located north of Great Falls, Montana, in Cascade, Chouteau, and Teton Counties (fig. 1). Benton Lake is formed by the accumulation of runoff within the closed basin, which encompasses about 146 square miles (mi²) and has little relief. Altitudes range from 3,615 to 3,850 feet (ft, above NGVD 29) in most of the basin. Hills bordering the north side of the basin rise to 4,020 ft.

Benton Lake NWR is managed by the USFWS. The refuge consists of 12,400 acres of land—6,800 acres in uplands and about 5,600 acres in wetlands. The wetlands of Benton Lake NWR are important as nesting and migration habitat for water birds. Thirty-five species of wetland-dependent birds nest at the refuge. On a per-acre basis, Benton Lake NWR is one of the most productive duck-producing areas in North America, with annual production ranging from 8,000 to 40,000 ducks. The refuge also provides spring and fall migration habitat for 53 bird species (Nimick and others, 1996).

Although established in 1929, Benton Lake NWR was not developed or staffed until 1961, when a pump station was constructed on Muddy Creek and the marsh area was divided into six wetland units (Units 1–6) by earthen dikes (fig. 1). Unit 4 subsequently was divided into three units (Units 4A–4C). Most of the water entering Benton Lake flows into Unit 1 from Lake Creek. This water then can be conveyed to the other wetland units by opening headgates to allow gravity flow directly to Unit 2 and then to Units 3–6 through the interunit canal. Historically, Units 1 and 2 have been managed to provide water deeper than about 3 ft all year (Nimick, 1997). Depending on water availability and goals of individual refuge managers, some or all of Units 3 to 6 have been flooded seasonally. When feasible to do so, these units have been filled in the spring to enhance nesting habitat for ducks and allowed to dry during the summer to prevent outbreaks of avian botulism. One or more of these units are flooded again in late summer and early fall for use by migrating birds and to store water for the following spring. When Units 3 to 6 are flooded, water depths in these units are shallow and the inundated area varies markedly with changes in water level.

Conceptual Model of the Hydrologic System

Water entering Benton Lake is derived from three sources: precipitation that falls on the lake; natural runoff that flows from the Benton Lake basin; and pumpage from Muddy Creek, whose flow consists almost entirely of irrigation drainage from the Greenfields Bench (fig. 1; Nimick and others, 1996). The water pumped from Muddy Creek is conveyed by a pipeline and canal to the Lake Creek channel, and the amount pumped varies year to year. The need for water from Muddy Creek is dependent on the quantity of runoff available from the Benton Lake basin and is evaluated annually to achieve optimum water levels while minimizing pumping costs. Managing water at Benton Lake NWR is complex because of the unpredictability of the timing and volume of inflows from natural runoff, the lack of a lake outlet to release excess water, and the varying seasonal needs for water levels necessary to optimize waterfowl habitat. Water is lost from Benton Lake only through evaporation. On average, the total annual volume of precipitation, pumped water, and runoff that falls on the lake evaporates. Therefore, water stored in the lake has no net long-term gain or loss.

Hydrologic Inputs

Precipitation data have been recorded at four weather stations near Benton Lake (table 1). Precipitation records from 1961 (when the wetland units were constructed) to the present are available for NOAA weather stations at Power 6 SE and Great Falls International Airport, which are 12 and 14 mi from the center of Benton Lake, respectively (fig. 1 and table 1). Precipitation records also are available for the period from 1983 to the present for the NOAA weather station at Carter 14 W, which is 11 mi from the center of Benton Lake. Precipitation data for these stations were retrieved for this report from NOAA's National Climatic Data Center Web site (National Oceanic and Atmospheric Administration, 2009). Finally, precipitation was measured during 1976–77 and 1979–81 by USFWS staff at the refuge headquarters, which is about 1.5 mi from the center of the wetlands (Steve Martin, Benton Lake NWR, written commun., 1995).

Mean annual precipitation for 1983–2008 (the period of record common to the three NOAA stations) is 12.98 inches (in.) at Carter 14 W, 11.70 in. at Power 6 SE, and 14.47 in. at Great Falls International Airport (table 2). The data for the combined mean precipitation for these three stations (table 3) appear to be the most useful for estimating precipitation that falls on Benton Lake for several reasons. First, these three stations surround and are about equidistant from Benton Lake.

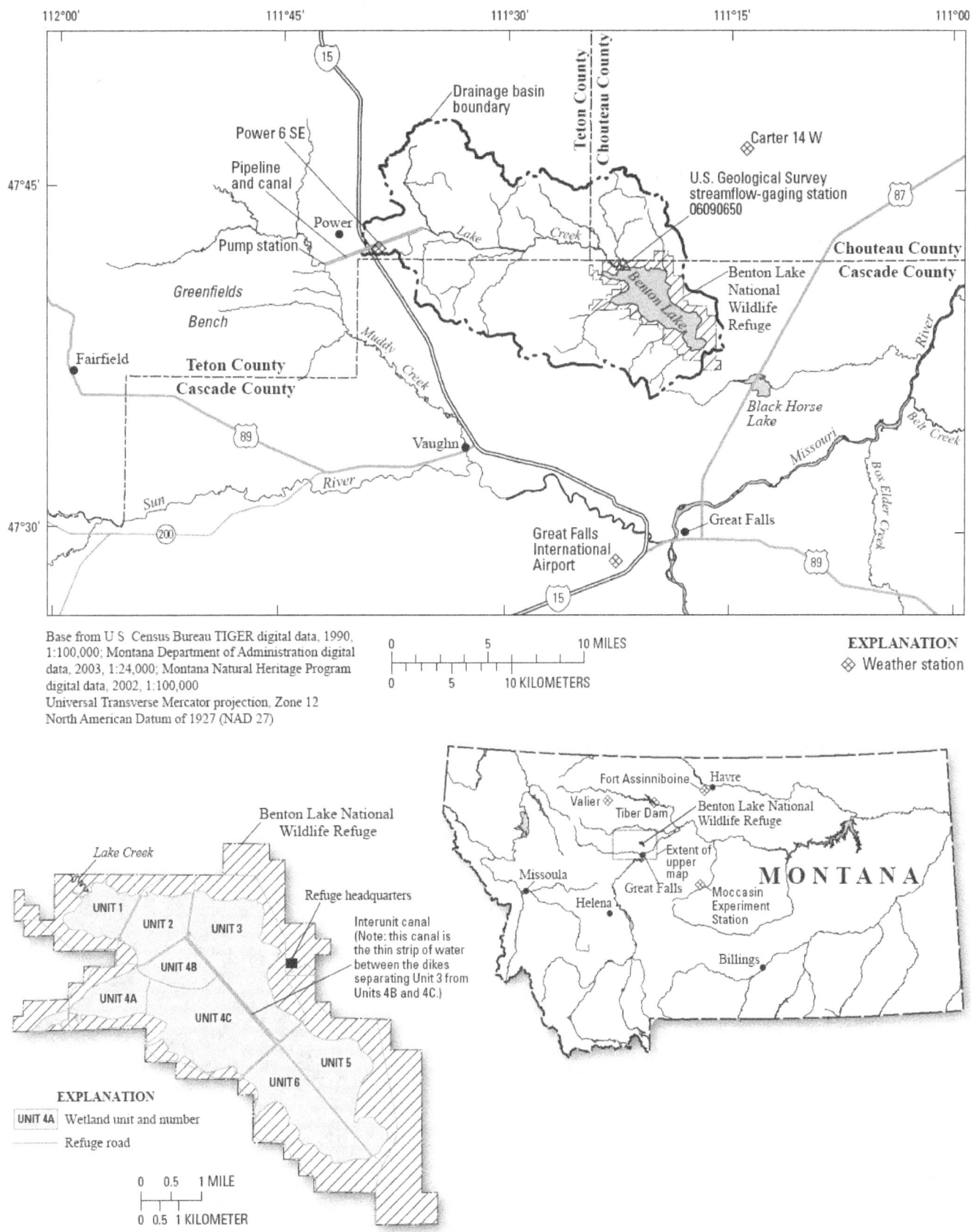

Figure 1. Locations of weather stations and streamflow-gaging station in the study area, Montana.

Second, although the precipitation data for the refuge head-quarters probably are most representative of precipitation that falls on Benton Lake because this precipitation station is closest to the wetlands, the period of record lacks data for recent years. The representativeness of the mean values for the three NOAA stations can be evaluated in more detail by comparing values for 1983–1995 to data collected at the refuge headquarters (table 4). Overall, the mean annual value at refuge headquarters (13.85 in.) is within 3 percent of the combined mean annual value for the three NOAA stations (13.51 in.), and the mean values for individual months at the refuge headquarters differed from the combined mean of the three NOAA stations by a maximum of only 0.21 in. Thus, the combined mean values for the three NOAA stations (table 3) are assumed to be applicable at Benton Lake.

For the purposes of the model, dry, average, and wet years are defined as years when annual precipitation equals (1) the mean annual precipitation (1983–2008) minus one standard deviation, (2) the mean annual precipitation, and (3) the mean annual precipitation plus one standard deviation, respectively. A very wet year is defined as a year when annual precipitation equals the mean annual precipitation plus three standard deviations (table 3). For calculations in the model of precipitation volumes, only precipitation that falls on inundated parts of a wetland unit is assumed to accumulate in that unit.

Water pumped from Muddy Creek provides the second hydrologic input to Benton Lake. The amount and timing of pumped water added to wetlands is based on management objectives, availability of water (derived from irrigation return flows) in Muddy Creek, and availability of funds for electricity. Since 1964, the actual volume of water pumped to Benton Lake was calculated from hours of pump operation and the rated capacities of the three pumps. The maximum theoretical pump capacity is 41.5 cubic feet per second, or 82.3 acre-feet/day. Since 1991, the volume of pumped water

also has been calculated by refuge staff from the streamflow data (fig. 2) collected at the seasonally operated gaging station on Lake Creek near the mouth of the stream (fig. 1) and information about when pumps were operated and when precipitation fell in the area. These volumes of pumped water are reported in annual water-use reports (Benton Lake National Wildlife Refuge, issued annually). Historical data on annual volumes of pumped water are listed in table 5.

Runoff derived from precipitation and snowmelt provides the third hydrologic input to Benton Lake. This runoff flows to Benton Lake primarily from Lake Creek but also as diffuse runoff from the ungaged parts of the basin that drain directly to the wetlands, particularly to Units 4 and 6. For the purposes of the model, runoff is assumed to enter any combination of one or more of the wetland units. Since 1964, monthly volumes of runoff that flowed to Benton Lake have been quantified by refuge staff from changes in water levels in each wetland unit. Water-level data collected before and after periods of runoff were used in conjunction with stage-capacity data for each unit to calculate the runoff volumes. Estimates of runoff included precipitation and evaporation that might have occurred during the period between the water-level measurements. Since 1991, the runoff that flows to Benton Lake from Lake Creek has been determined by refuge staff as the difference between the total flow measured at the Lake Creek gaging station minus the flow estimated to have been water pumped from Muddy Creek. In addition, diffuse runoff flowing from ungaged parts of the Benton Lake basin since 1991 was estimated as the difference between total runoff estimated from changes in water levels of each wetland unit and runoff determined from the gaging-station records. The annual water-use reports (Benton Lake National Wildlife Refuge, issued annually) document the monthly volumes of runoff flowing to Benton Lake from ungaged parts of the basin and, after 1990, the monthly volumes of gaged flow in Lake Creek attributable to runoff.

Table 1. Weather stations that have recorded precipitation near Benton Lake, Montana.

[Abbreviations: NGVD 29, National Geodetic Vertical Datum of 1929; NOAA, National Oceanic and Atmospheric Administration; NA, not applicable]

Weather station	Period of record	Altitude (feet above NGVD 29)	Latitude (degrees, minutes)	Longitude (degrees, minutes)	NOAA weather station number	Distance from center of Benton Lake (miles)
Benton Lake National Wildlife Refuge Headquarters	1976–77, 1979–81	3,660	47°41′ N	111°19′ W	NA	1.5
Power 6 SE	1953–present	3,750	47°39′ N	111°36′ W	246700	12
Great Falls International Airport	1937–present	3,664	47°28′ N	111°23′ W	243751	14
Carter 14 W	1983–present	3,450	47°48′ N	111°13′ W	241525	11

Table 2. Monthly precipitation recorded at three weather stations near Benton Lake, Montana, 1983–2008.

[Precipitation in inches. Data from National Oceanic and Atmospheric Administration (2009)]

Year or statistic	Jan.	Feb.	Mar.	Apr.	May	June	July	Aug.	Sept.	Oct.	Nov.	Dec.	Annual
					Power 6 SE, station number 246700								
1983	0.07	0.08	1.38	0.38	1.36	1.45	3.14	1.01	0.95	0.74	0.91	0.57	12.04
1984	.55	.50	.30	.73	1.05	.94	.39	.89	.83	1.23	.05	.79	8.25
1985	.12	.34	.75	.69	1.75	.71	.38	4.44	3.45	.92	1.16	.40	15.11
1986	.29	.86	.23	1.59	1.16	.60	.50	0.80	3.86	.36	.53	.32	11.10
1987	.06	.12	1.57	.37	2.15	.50	2.54	2.10	.35	.03	.30	.16	10.25
1988	.58	.35	.19	.17	1.98	1.57	.86	.10	1.58	.42	.18	.51	8.49
1989	.71	1.01	1.08	1.49	1.75	1.84	2.04	4.61	.88	.59	.63	.79	17.42
1990	.19	.12	1.18	1.00	2.17	.51	.88	2.19	.04	.03	.39	.42	9.12
1991	.52	.39	1.24	1.76	2.07	4.43	.62	.43	.52	.48	.46	.08	13.00
1992	.26	.20	.31	1.12	1.55	2.52	2.07	1.11	.29	1.92	.47	.32	12.14
1993	.71	.45	.45	2.87	2.35	2.58	5.51	3.17	1.61	.84	.74	.21	21.49
1994	.34	.59	.11	1.69	1.05	.55	.50	.86	.28	1.06	.26	.23	7.52
1995	.02	.13	.24	1.18	2.91	3.06	2.03	.56	1.48	.91	.28	.17	12.97
1996	.46	.20	.69	.83	2.75	1.12	.40	.51	1.56	.43	.58	.99	10.52
1997	.26	.31	.44	1.08	2.29	1.53	1.40	.95	.23	.45	.14	.20	9.28
1998	.55	.14	.60	.36	2.02	4.65	1.36	1.29	1.50	.67	.95	.20	14.29
1999	.28	.32	.50	1.23	1.91	1.57	.56	2.30	1.64	.83	.40	.04	11.58
2000	.40	.68	.44	.29	1.52	2.27	.33	.25	.97	1.33	.35	.23	9.06
2001	.36	.36	.34	.78	.31	1.88	1.67	.62	.97	.21	.17	.07	7.74
2002	.22	.17	.56	.38	.98	5.25	.70	2.64	1.59	.56	.35	.31	13.71
2003	.14	.29	.51	1.61	1.40	2.07	.21	.77	1.45	.66	.22	.21	9.54
2004	.17	.07	.13	1.53	1.92	2.65	.27	2.95	1.19	.96	.08	.40	12.32
2005	.34	.03	.93	1.20	1.33	4.61	.03	1.24	1.07	.49	.72	.19	12.18
2006	.32	.22	.94	2.12	2.12	4.26	.38	.88	1.10	.73	.25	.40	13.72
2007	.13	.64	.05	1.85	1.77	1.26	.52	.25	1.50	.61	.31	.06	8.95
2008	.40	.24	.25	.55	3.56	2.03	1.11	.60	2.08	.20	.51	.79	12.32
Mean	.33	.34	.59	1.11	1.81	2.17	1.17	1.44	1.27	.68	.44	.35	11.70
Standard deviation	.19	.25	.42	.66	.68	1.42	1.20	1.24	.88	.42	.28	.25	3.17
Maximum	.71	1.01	1.57	2.87	3.56	5.25	5.51	4.61	3.86	1.92	1.16	.99	21.49
Minimum	.02	.03	.05	.17	.31	.50	.03	.10	.04	.03	.05	.04	7.52

Table 2. Monthly precipitation recorded at three weather stations near Benton Lake, Montana, 1983–2008.—Continued

[Precipitation in inches. Data from National Oceanic and Atmospheric Administration (2009)]

Year or statistic	Jan.	Feb.	Mar.	Apr.	May	June	July	Aug.	Sept.	Oct.	Nov.	Dec.	Annual
Great Falls International Airport, station number 243751													
1983	0.10	0.33	1.61	0.26	1.34	3.03	3.78	1.10	1.89	0.77	1.28	0.70	16.19
1984	.72	.69	1.31	.94	1.34	2.10	.05	1.01	.71	1.20	.49	1.25	11.81
1985	.35	.22	1.02	.41	3.28	.58	.47	4.90	3.23	1.10	1.16	.47	17.19
1986	.57	.75	.10	2.83	1.74	1.72	1.67	.81	1.52	.90	.45	.27	13.33
1987	.05	.24	1.81	.64	2.63	1.33	3.05	2.43	1.30	.02	.30	.24	14.04
1988	.76	.47	.44	.77	1.60	1.42	1.82	.26	2.33	.66	.30	.97	11.80
1989	.96	1.19	1.38	2.41	2.41	1.70	3.03	4.88	1.87	.41	.81	1.32	22.37
1990	.29	.17	1.69	.84	3.97	1.23	1.03	3.19	.09	.13	.70	.73	14.06
1991	.63	.21	1.21	1.54	1.54	4.15	.75	1.35	1.00	.81	.77	.08	14.04
1992	.48	.23	.43	1.32	2.14	3.22	1.81	1.37	.25	2.61	.29	.31	14.46
1993	1.17	.70	.86	3.16	2.74	2.58	4.68	3.04	1.71	1.10	.97	.30	23.01
1994	.47	.53	.20	1.90	1.81	1.56	.72	.60	.35	1.77	.42	.24	10.57
1995	.05	.15	.82	2.17	3.11	2.91	3.36	.55	1.20	.62	.35	.14	15.43
1996	.49	.26	.83	1.40	2.57	1.14	.17	.67	1.47	.54	.35	1.25	11.14
1997	.27	.32	.62	1.27	2.89	3.49	1.88	1.61	.27	.91	.18	.33	14.04
1998	.72	.42	1.10	.42	3.08	5.18	1.73	1.72	1.00	.80	.96	.22	17.35
1999	.33	.36	.53	1.43	2.29	1.67	.81	2.18	1.72	.67	.45	.03	12.47
2000	.34	.69	.74	.33	2.10	1.55	1.04	.12	1.32	1.34	.49	.19	10.25
2001	.65	.39	.51	1.10	.51	1.79	2.74	.26	1.50	.33	.14	.39	10.31
2002	.30	.26	.70	.42	1.61	5.03	1.50	2.49	1.65	.47	.27	.29	14.99
2003	.12	.61	.49	1.78	2.11	1.85	.18	1.31	1.13	.27	.18	.11	10.14
2004	.23	.06	.29	1.06	2.91	2.82	.42	2.55	1.99	1.05	.16	.43	13.97
2005	.16	.01	.94	1.20	1.07	6.85	.10	.97	1.68	.69	1.69	.29	15.65
2006	.71	.44	1.70	2.88	2.64	4.24	.27	1.33	1.82	1.48	.43	.59	18.53
2007	.28	1.53	.25	2.35	2.81	1.00	.13	.24	1.71	.68	.76	.12	11.86
2008	.84	.43	.35	1.51	3.82	3.08	1.25	1.31	1.87	.53	.74	1.43	17.16
Mean	.46	.45	.84	1.40	2.31	2.59	1.48	1.63	1.41	.84	.58	.49	14.47
Standard deviation	.29	.34	.50	.83	.84	1.51	1.28	1.29	.70	.54	.39	.42	3.39
Maximum	1.17	1.53	1.81	3.16	3.97	6.85	4.68	4.90	3.23	2.61	1.69	1.43	23.01
Minimum	.05	.01	.10	.26	.51	.58	.05	.12	.09	.02	.14	.03	10.14

Table 2. Monthly precipitation recorded at three weather stations near Benton Lake, Montana, 1983–2008.—Continued

[Precipitation in inches. Data from National Oceanic and Atmospheric Administration (2009)]

Year or statistic	Jan.	Feb.	Mar.	Apr.	May	June	July	Aug.	Sept.	Oct.	Nov.	Dec.	Annual
Carter 14 W, station number 241525													
1983	0.05	0.15	1.20	0.26	1.47	3.21	3.40	0.41	1.44	0.38	0.68	0.44	13.09
1984	.38	.61	.32	.54	1.57	1.76	.05	1.26	.86	1.39	.02	.44	9.20
1985	.18	.15	.94	.40	2.12	.55	.06	5.43	4.22	1.02	1.44	.40	16.91
1986	.34	.91	.22	1.84	2.01	1.33	1.12	2.27	2.86	.71	.57	.19	14.37
1987	.01	.12	1.39	.61	2.47	.68	2.16	2.31	.84	0.00	.15	.03	10.77
1988	.50	.19	.51	.42	1.50	1.43	1.15	.10	2.88	.35	.17	.59	9.79
1989	.60	.92	.76	2.58	1.87	1.96	2.82	3.97	1.12	.41	.72	1.17	18.90
1990	.19	.05	1.47	.80	2.52	1.14	1.35	2.49	0.00	.02	.41	.30	10.74
1991	.47	.29	.78	2.46	2.19	4.87	.43	.75	.58	.69	.49	0.00	14.00
1992	.32	.15	.24	1.07	1.25	1.83	2.27	1.36	.33	2.13	.23	.25	11.43
1993	.61	.64	.66	1.85	1.71	2.78	5.67	2.38	1.02	.79	.78	.16	19.05
1994	.02	.04	.61	1.18	3.56	2.87	1.94	.42	.77	.80	.48	.27	12.96
1995	.37	.29	.03	1.45	1.43	1.58	.30	.43	.38	1.36	.46	.26	8.34
1996	.59	.37	.80	1.04	2.75	.90	.14	.50	1.09	.35	.40	.99	9.92
1997	.30	.32	.49	1.12	1.67	1.37	1.12	1.12	.46	.66	.32	.14	9.09
1998	.52	.06	.68	.45	1.22	2.97	3.48	1.72	.90	.61	1.20	.18	13.99
1999	.38	.39	.73	1.07	2.29	2.57	.74	2.85	1.99	1.09	.63	.08	14.81
2000	.34	.68	.81	.42	2.65	1.59	.83	.20	1.15	1.27	.58	.39	10.91
2001	.36	.50	.34	1.26	.16	1.52	2.00	.21	.84	.33	.34	.06	7.92
2002	.21	.31	.82	.50	2.28	5.35	.54	2.66	1.53	.71	.37	.21	15.49
2003	.14	.60	.35	1.52	2.06	1.75	0.00	.93	1.46	1.12	.37	.48	10.78
2004	.64	.03	.16	1.63	3.22	2.08	.18	2.71	1.51	1.27	.05	.41	13.89
2005	.32	.01	1.45	1.19	1.48	4.81	.26	1.63	1.20	1.04	1.35	.22	14.96
2006	.40	.33	1.39	1.90	3.08	3.98	.52	.88	1.16	1.57	.27	.84	16.32
2007	.18	1.22	.07	2.19	2.16	1.58	.18	.42	1.80	.73	.20	.03	10.76
2008	.34	.34	.56	1.88	4.82	3.38	2.70	1.29	1.74	.17	.65	1.26	19.13
Mean	.34	.37	.68	1.22	2.14	2.30	1.36	1.57	1.31	.81	.51	.38	12.98
Standard deviation	.18	.31	.43	.68	.90	1.31	1.39	1.29	.91	.51	.36	.34	3.33
Maximum	.64	1.22	1.47	2.58	4.82	5.35	5.67	5.43	4.22	2.13	1.44	1.26	19.13
Minimum	.01	.01	.03	.26	.16	.55	0.00	.10	0.00	0.00	.02	0.00	7.92

Table 3. Combined means of monthly precipitation values recorded at weather stations at Carter 14 W, Power 6 SE, and Great Falls International Airport, Montana, 1983–2008.

[Precipitation in inches. Data from National Oceanic and Atmospheric Administration (2009). Annual precipitation for wet and dry years computed as mean annual plus and minus, respectively, one standard deviation. Annual precipitation for very wet years computed as mean annual plus three standard deviations. Monthly precipitation values for wet and dry years are defined as the mean monthly precipitation values for 1983–2008 plus and minus, respectively, a percentage of the 1983–2008 mean monthly, where the percentage is the percent difference of the annual standard deviation from the mean annual. Monthly precipitation values for very wet years are defined as the mean monthly precipitation values for 1983–2008 plus a percentage of the 1983–2008 mean monthly, where the percentage is three times the percent difference of the annual standard deviation from the mean annual]

Year or statistic	Jan.	Feb.	Mar.	Apr.	May	June	July	Aug.	Sept.	Oct.	Nov.	Dec.	Annual
1983	0.07	0.19	1.40	0.30	1.39	2.56	3.44	0.84	1.43	0.63	0.96	0.57	13.77
1984	.55	.60	.64	.74	1.32	1.60	.16	1.05	.80	1.27	.19	.83	9.75
1985	.22	.24	.90	.50	2.38	.61	.30	4.92	3.63	1.01	1.25	.42	16.40
1986	.40	.84	.18	2.09	1.64	1.22	1.10	1.29	2.75	.66	.52	.26	12.93
1987	.04	.16	1.59	.54	2.42	.84	2.58	2.28	.83	.02	.25	.14	11.69
1988	.61	.34	.38	.45	1.69	1.47	1.28	.15	2.26	.48	.22	.69	10.03
1989	.76	1.04	1.07	2.16	2.01	1.83	2.63	4.49	1.29	.47	.72	1.09	19.56
1990	.22	.11	1.45	.88	2.89	.96	1.09	2.62	.04	.06	.50	.48	11.31
1991	.54	.30	1.08	1.92	1.93	4.48	.60	.84	.70	.66	.57	.05	13.68
1992	.35	.19	.33	1.17	1.65	2.52	2.05	1.28	.29	2.22	.33	.29	12.68
1993	.83	.60	.66	2.63	2.27	2.65	5.29	2.86	1.45	.91	.83	.22	21.18
1994	.28	.39	.31	1.59	2.14	1.66	1.05	.63	.47	1.21	.39	.25	10.35
1995	.15	.19	.36	1.60	2.48	2.52	1.90	.51	1.02	.96	.36	.19	12.25
1996	.51	.28	.77	1.09	2.69	1.05	.24	.56	1.37	.44	.44	1.08	10.53
1997	.28	.32	.52	1.16	2.28	2.13	1.47	1.23	.32	.67	.21	.22	10.80
1998	.60	.21	.79	.41	2.11	4.27	2.19	1.58	1.13	.69	1.04	.20	15.21
1999	.33	.36	.59	1.24	2.16	1.94	.70	2.44	1.78	.86	.49	.05	12.95
2000	.36	.68	.66	.35	2.09	1.80	.73	.19	1.15	1.31	.47	.27	10.07
2001	.46	.42	.40	1.05	.33	1.73	2.14	.36	1.10	.29	.22	.17	8.66
2002	.24	.25	.69	.43	1.62	5.21	.91	2.60	1.59	.58	.33	.27	14.73
2003	.13	.50	.45	1.64	1.86	1.89	.13	1.00	1.35	.68	.26	.27	10.15
2004	.35	.05	.19	1.41	2.68	2.52	.29	2.74	1.56	1.09	.10	.41	13.39
2005	.27	.02	1.11	1.20	1.29	5.42	.13	1.28	1.32	.74	1.25	.23	14.26
2006	.48	.33	1.34	2.30	2.61	4.16	.39	1.03	1.36	1.26	.32	.61	16.19
2007	.20	1.13	.12	2.13	2.25	1.28	.28	.30	1.67	.67	.42	.07	10.52
2008	.53	.34	.39	1.31	4.07	2.83	1.69	1.07	1.90	.30	.63	1.16	16.20
Mean	.38	.39	.71	1.24	2.09	2.35	1.34	1.54	1.33	.78	.51	.40	13.05
Standard deviation	.20	.28	.42	.68	.68	1.33	1.22	1.25	.76	.46	.32	.32	3.08
Minimum	.04	.02	.12	.30	.33	.61	.13	.15	.04	.02	.10	.05	8.66
Maximum	.83	1.13	1.59	2.63	4.07	5.42	5.29	4.92	3.63	2.22	1.25	1.16	21.18
Dry year	.29	.30	.54	.95	1.59	1.80	1.02	1.18	1.02	.59	.39	.31	9.97
Wet year	.46	.48	.87	1.53	2.58	2.91	1.65	1.91	1.64	.96	.63	.50	16.13
Very wet year	.64	.66	1.21	2.12	3.56	4.02	2.28	2.64	2.27	1.32	.87	.69	22.28

Annual volumes of runoff from 1964 through 2008 were highly varied and ranged from 0 to 19,200 acre-feet (acre-ft), with a mean of 2,458 acre-ft (table 5). The reliability of this long-term estimate of runoff was supported by results from an estimation equation (Omang and Parrett, 1984) applicable to central and eastern Montana that gave a similar estimated mean of 3,110 acre-ft (Charles Parrett, U.S. Geological Survey, written commun., 1992). However, the median annual runoff (837 acre-ft; table 5) is much less than the mean annual value and probably is more indicative of the typical amount of runoff that is likely to occur in any one year. In addition, the amount of runoff appears to have decreased with time. The median annual runoff for 1964–89 was 1,855 acre-ft, whereas the median for 1990–2008 was 490 acre-ft.

Monthly values of runoff derived from Lake Creek and ungaged drainages are listed in table 6 for 1991–2008. Runoff is more likely to occur during the spring (March–June) than later in the year. On average, about 40 percent of the runoff each year flows to Benton Lake in June.

Table 4. Historical precipitation data recorded at Benton Lake National Wildlife Refuge and at three weather stations near Benton Lake, Montana, 1983–95.

[Precipitation in inches. Data from National Oceanic and Atmospheric Administration (2009) and Steve Martin (Benton Lake National Wildlife Refuge, unpub. data, 1995)]

Statistic	Jan.	Feb.	Mar.	Apr.	May	June	July	Aug.	Sept.	Oct.	Nov.	Dec.	Annual
Benton Lake National Wildlife Refuge Headquarters													
Mean	0.51	0.45	0.94	1.21	2.22	1.88	1.60	1.67	1.22	0.73	0.51	0.50	13.85
Standard deviation	.39	.38	.66	.79	.97	1.16	1.20	1.51	1.10	.55	.45	.43	3.99
Maximum	1.32	1.26	2.86	2.74	4.75	4.38	4.12	5.68	4.09	1.96	1.72	1.69	21.71
Minimum	.00	.00	.08	.00	.62	.03	.00	.05	.00	.00	.00	.00	8.36
Carter 14 W													
Mean	.31	.35	.70	1.19	1.97	2.00	1.75	1.81	1.33	.77	.51	.35	13.04
Standard deviation	.21	.31	.45	.79	.62	1.18	1.59	1.56	1.23	.60	.36	.30	3.52
Maximum	.61	.92	1.47	2.58	3.56	4.87	5.67	5.43	4.22	2.13	1.44	1.17	19.05
Minimum	.01	.04	.03	.26	1.25	.55	.05	.10	.00	.00	.02	.00	8.34
Power SE 6													
Mean	.34	.40	.69	1.16	1.79	1.64	1.65	1.71	1.24	.73	.49	.38	12.22
Standard deviation	.25	.29	.52	.74	.55	1.22	1.49	1.50	1.19	.51	.31	.23	3.97
Maximum	.71	1.01	1.57	2.87	2.91	4.43	5.51	4.61	3.86	1.92	1.16	.79	21.49
Minimum	.02	.08	.11	.17	1.05	.50	.38	.10	.04	.03	.05	.08	7.52
Great Falls International Airport													
Mean	.51	.45	.99	1.48	2.28	2.12	2.02	1.96	1.34	.93	.64	.54	15.25
Standard deviation	.35	.31	.57	.95	.83	1.00	1.44	1.59	.89	.68	.34	.42	3.76
Maximum	1.17	1.19	1.81	3.16	3.97	4.15	4.68	4.90	3.23	2.61	1.28	1.32	23.01
Minimum	.05	.15	.10	.26	1.34	.58	.05	.26	.09	.02	.29	.08	10.57
Combined means—Carter 14 W, Power 6 SE, and Great Falls International Airport													
Mean	.39	.40	.80	1.27	2.02	1.92	1.81	1.83	1.30	.81	.54	.42	13.51

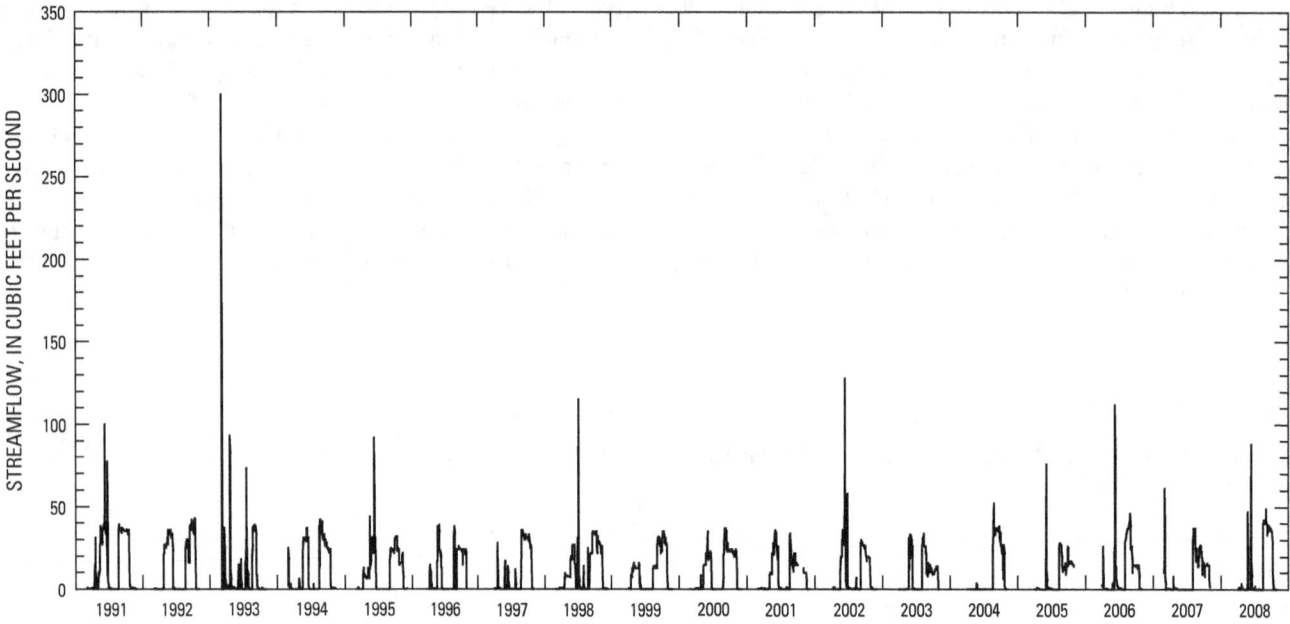

Figure 2.   Daily mean streamflow at Lake Creek near Power, Montana (U.S. Geological Survey streamflow-gaging station 06090650), 1991–2008. Gaging station was operated seasonally, and no data are available each year typically for November through February or March.

For simulating future scenarios, being able to estimate the amount of runoff generated by precipitation is essential. However, estimating how much runoff flows to Benton Lake from precipitation events on the basis of historical data is imprecise. A plot (fig. 3) of monthly precipitation (table 3) and monthly runoff (table 6) shows a fair relation, and this relation is used in the model to compute runoff. March data were not included in this analysis because runoff during March typically results from snowmelt runoff and not in response to precipitation events. About 2 to 3 in. of rain typically is needed in a month to produce substantial runoff (greater than 200 acre-ft).

Hydrologic Outputs

Water is assumed to be lost from the wetlands solely by evaporation from plants and water surfaces. In addition, water could be lost from wetland units by downward percolation to groundwater. However, Nimick and others (1996) concluded that little water is lost from Benton Lake to groundwater because of the relatively impermeable glacial-lake sediment that underlies the wetlands. An additional loss of wetland water could occur when a dry wetland unit is flooded, particularly a unit that may have been dry for a long (multiyear) period, as some of the water used to flood the unit may be lost to resaturation of the desiccated bottom sediment. However, this resaturation loss is assumed to be zero in the model because no data are available to quantify this potential type of water loss and loss to sediment resaturation is thought to be minimal when units are flooded every year.

Water loss through evaporation from lakes is dependent on the relatively complex interplay of solar radiation, temperature, wind speed, and relative humidity. Typically, evaporation varies from year to year but the relative amount of variation generally is less than for precipitation and runoff (Dunne and Leopold, 1978). Evaporation data collected with a Class A evaporation pan have been recorded at the refuge headquarters and at four NOAA weather stations 47 to 91 mi from Benton Lake (fig. 1 and tables 7 and 8). For the refuge headquarters, pan-evaporation data are available only for 5 years (1976–77, 1979–81), and monthly values are recorded in annual wateruse reports (Benton Lake National Wildlife Refuge, issued annually). For the NOAA stations, data collection was terminated in the 1970s at the two stations closest to Benton Lake, whereas data have been collected from 1948 to the present (2008, for this study) at Moccasin Experiment Station and Fort Assinniboine, the two more distant stations.

The pan-evaporation data from Fort Assinniboine (table 9) appear to be the most representative and complete for use in understanding evaporation from Benton Lake for several reasons. First, the more recent data (post 1965) show that the pan-evaporation values for the April–September period at four of the five stations are similar, ranging from 36.51 to 37.51 in., and indicate that pan evaporation measured at the fifth station (Moccasin Experiment Station) likely is not representative of Benton Lake (table 8). The pan-evaporation data for Tiber Dam and Valier appear to be representative of Benton Lake, but were not used in the model owing to the lack of recent data. Similarly, the pan-evaporation data for the refuge headquarters were not used owing to the lack of

Table 5. Annual volumes of pumped water and runoff entering Benton Lake, Montana, 1964–2008.

[Runoff to Benton Lake was determined by subtracting pumped water (estimated from pump-capacity data for 1964–90 or measured at the Lake Creek near Power (06090650) streamflow-gaging station for 1991–2008) from the total inflow (estimated from water-level data) to Benton Lake. Data compiled from annual water-use reports (Benton Lake National Wildlife Refuge, issued annually). Symbol: --, no data]

Year	Pumped water (acre-feet)		Runoff (acre-feet)		Year	Pumped water (acre-feet)		Runoff (acre-feet)	
	Measured at Lake Creek gaging station	Estimated from pump-capacity data	Measured at Lake Creek gaging station	Estimated from water-level and pumped-water data		Measured at Lake Creek gaging station	Estimated from pump-capacity data	Measured at Lake Creek gaging station	Estimated from water-level and pumped-water data
1964	--	--	--	7,125	1987	--	7,987	--	350
1965	--	--	--	2,560	1988	--	7,517	--	208
1966	--	--	--	2,530	1989	--	212	--	9,710
1967	--	--	--	0	1990	--	4,797	--	1,056
1968	--	--	--	0	1991	7,064	8,028	719	298
1969	--	--	--	9,600	1992	6,574	7,276	21	0
1970	--	3,670	--	3,000	1993	1,718	1,932	2,955	70
1971	--	6,371	--	0	1994	5,611	5,800	227	0
1972	--	9,079	--	990	1995	5,559	--	344	55
1973	--	6,643	--	0	1996	4,067	3,969	305	85
1974	--	5,897	--	334	1997	3,428	--	337	--
1975	--	0	--	13,933	1998	5,693	6,684	622	128
1976	--	2,978	--	400	1999	5,033	6,513	122	0
1977	--	4,167	--	0	2000	5,386	5,790	53	0
1978	--	0	--	19,200	2001	4,410	5,720	51	0
1979	--	68	--	12,100	2002	3,975	5,959	610	0
1980	--	2,000	--	1,100	2003	3,868	5,509	4	0
1981	--	3,650	--	3,813	2004	3,985	4,795	73	0
1982	--	3,037	--	4,132	2005	2,849	3,397	422	463
1983	--	2,822	--	1,763	2006	3,951	4,526	827	1,592
1984	--	4,790	--	1,947	2007	3,542	--	486	121
1985	--	6,380	--	1,157	2008	4,204	--	673	164
1986	--	3,376	--	4,759	Mean	[1]4,266		[2]2,458	
					Median	[1]4,067		[2]837	

[1]Computed using estimates from pump-capacity data for 1970–90 and amount measured at gaging station for 1991–2008.

[2]Computed using estimates from water-level and pump-capacity data for 1964–90 and amount measured at gaging station for 1991–2008.

recent data. The representativeness of the Fort Assinniboine data can be evaluated in more detail by comparing values for the 5 years during 1976–1981 when data were collected at refuge headquarters (table 10). Overall, the total of the mean monthly values for April–September at the refuge head-quarters (37.47 in.) is about 4 percent higher than the value (35.89 in.) at Fort Assinniboine, whereas mean monthly values for individual months over the 1976–81 period varied by as much as 19 percent. Thus, the Fort Assinniboine data (table 9) are assumed to be applicable at Benton Lake. On the basis of data for 1966–2008, mean monthly pan evaporation at Fort Assinniboine ranged from 4.50 in. for April and September to 8.16 in. for July (table 9). Most monthly values have a range (mean ± 2 standard deviations) of about 3–4 in. for the cooler months (April–June and September) and about 5 in. for the hotter summer months (July and August).

Table 6.   Monthly volumes of inflows of pumped water and runoff to Benton Lake, Montana, 1991–2008.

[Volumes in acre-feet. Symbol: --, no data]

Year	Mar.	Apr.	May	June	July	Aug.	Sept.	Oct.	Nov.	Total
Pumped water measured at Lake Creek near Power (06090650) streamflow-gaging station										
1991	0	0	1,570	1,287	0	806	2,120	1,260	21	7,064
1992	0	401	1,900	635	0	766	1,960	912	--	6,574
1993	0	0	0		0	923	795	--	--	1,718
1994	0	0	827	1,054	8	1,422	1,676	624	--	5,611
1995	0	356	1,093	849	0	77	1,490	1,370	324	5,559
1996	0	0	629	530	0.3	448	1,190	1,270	0	4,067
1997	0	0	0	0	0	672	1,860	896	0	3,428
1998	0	241	751	734	0	0	1,520	1,840	607	5,693
1999	0	357	821	36	0	478	1,474	1,834	33	5,033
2000	0	30	758	842	0.8	365	1,710	1,380	300	5,386
2001	0	0	1,040	1,056	0	619	1,010	530	155	4,410
2002	0	0	771	783	0	0	1,420	988	13	3,975
2003	0	0	391	741	0	1410	674	652	--	3,868
2004	0	0	0	0	0	885	2,100	1,000	--	3,985
2005	0	0	0	0	0	933	811	986	119	2,849
2006	0	0	0	364	0	1,979	1,110	498	--	3,951
2007	0	0	0	0	0	1,490	1,190	862	--	3,542
2008	0	0	0	0	0	1,230	2,270	704	--	4,204
Runoff measured at Lake Creek near Power (06090650) streamflow-gaging station										
1991	26	189	0	493	11	0	0	0	0	719
1992	12	9	0	0	0	0	0	0	0	21
1993	1,530	510	30	242	595	36	0	12	0	2,955
1994	173	45	9	0	0	0	0	0	0	227
1995	8.5	24	87	221	3.2	0	0	0	0	344
1996	--	194	111	0	0	0	0	0	0	305
1997	--	149	74	81	33	0	0	0	0	337
1998	14	16	0	145	325	122	0	0	0	622
1999	--	40	24	22	0	4	16	16	0	122
2000	3.4	14	6	30	0	0	0	0	0	53
2001	27	13	0	4	2.3	5	0	0	0	51
2002	--	16	12	547	13	22	0	0	0	610
2003	--	0.6	0.1	3.6	0	0	0	0	0	4
2004	--	2.9	16	3.2	0	51	0	0	0	73
2005	--	14	3.5	360	2.2	0	42	0	0	422
2006	--	121	20	589	16	81	0	0	0	827
2007	432	43	11	0.2	0	0	0	0	0	486
2008	--	41	195	424	13	0	0	0	0	673

Table 6.   Monthly volumes of inflows of pumped water and runoff to Benton Lake, Montana, 1991–2008.—Continued

[Volumes in acre-feet. Symbol: --, no data]

Year	Mar.	Apr.	May	June	July	Aug.	Sept.	Oct.	Nov.	Total
				Estimated runoff from ungaged drainages						
1991	0	298	0	0	0	0	0	0	0	298
1992	0	0	0	0	0	0	0	0	0	0
1993	70	0	0	0	0	0	0	0	0	70
1994	0	0	0	0	0	0	0	0	0	0
1995	0	0	33	22	0	0	0	0	0	55
1996	45	40	0	0	0	0	0	0	0	85
1997	--	--	--	--	--	--	--	--	--	--
1998	0	0	0	0	128	0	0	0	0	128
1999	0	0	0	0	0	0	0	0	0	0
2000	0	0	0	0	0	0	0	0	0	0
2001	0	0	0	0	0	0	0	0	0	0
2002	0	0	0	0	0	0	0	0	0	0
2003	0	0	0	0	0	0	0	0	0	0
2004	0	0	0	0	0	0	0	0	0	0
2005	0	0	0	463	0	0	0	0	0	463
2006	0	0	0	1,592	0	0	0	0	0	1,592
2007	121	0	0	0	0	0	0	0	0	121
2008	0	0	0	164	0	0	0	0	0	164

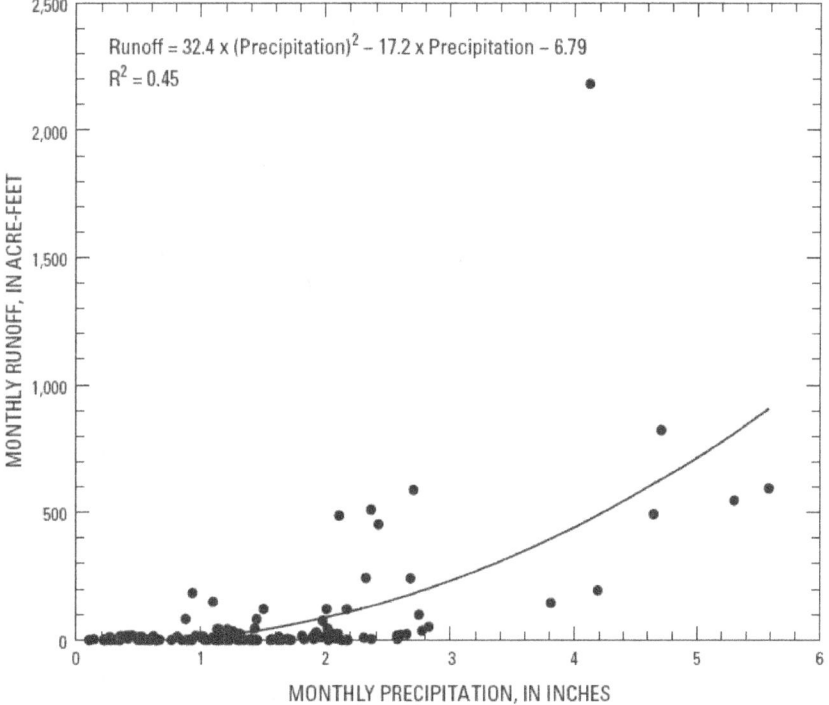

$$\text{Runoff} = 32.4 \times (\text{Precipitation})^2 - 17.2 \times \text{Precipitation} - 6.79$$
$$R^2 = 0.45$$

Figure 3.   Relation of combined mean monthly precipitation (April–October) at three weather stations to monthly runoff volume, Benton Lake, Montana, 1991–2008. See figure 1 for location of weather stations.

Table 7.   Weather stations that have recorded pan evaporation near Benton Lake, Montana.

[Abbreviations: NGVD 29, National Geodetic Vertical Datum of 1929; NOAA, National Oceanic and Atmospheric Administration. Symbol: --, no data]

Weather station	Period of record	Altitude (feet above NGVD 29)	Latitude (degrees, minutes)	Longitude (degrees, minutes)	NOAA weather station number	Distance from center of Benton Lake (miles)
Benton Lake National Wildlife Refuge Headquarters	1976–77, 1979–81	3,660	47°41′ N	111°19′ W	--	1.5
Tiber Dam	1953–75	2,850	48°19′ N	111°05′ W	248233	47
Valier	1916–78	3,810	48°19′ N	112°15′ W	248501	62
Moccasin Experiment Station	1948–present	4,300	47°03′ N	109°57′ W	245761	78
Fort Assinniboine	1948–present	2,613	48°30′ N	109°48′ W	243110	91

Pan-evaporation data are not available for October at Fort Assinniboine. However, October data are available from the 5-year record for Benton Lake (table 10). In the absence of a longer period of record for October pan evaporation, the mean monthly value of 3.37 in. from Benton Lake is assumed to be representative for October for all years. This value may be low because pan evaporation typically was not measured during the entire month at the refuge headquarters.

The amount of evaporation that occurs per unit area of open water is different for large lakes and Class A evaporation pans, which are 4 ft in diameter. Typically, the evaporation rate from a Class A pan is larger than from a lake because the pan receives large amounts of energy from solar radiation and from conduction through the base and sides of the pan. Therefore, a coefficient typically is applied to pan-evaporation data when using these data to estimate lake evaporation. Typically, pan-evaporation coefficients range from about 0.6 to 0.8 (Dunne and Leopold, 1978). Farnsworth and others (1982) mapped pan-evaporation coefficients for the continental United States; the value shown for the Benton Lake area is 0.73.

Other Considerations

The interunit canal (fig. 1) is important for transferring water among wetland units but is considered relatively unimportant in terms of the water management because its surface area (30 acres) is small in comparison to the total area of wetlands (about 5,600 acres), and therefore relatively little water typically is added by precipitation (less than 50 acre-ft annually) or lost to evaporation (less than 100 acre-ft annually) relative to the wetland units. In addition, water-level fluctuations are small in the canal, thus changes in storage in the canal are not included in the model.

Water balances over the winter period (November–March) are difficult to quantify because water in the wetland units is frozen and water-level data measured at ice-free monitoring sites are not available. The wetland units typically are completely ice covered from mid to late November through mid to late March. In addition, the streamflow-gaging station on Lake Creek was not operated during these winter periods.

For the model, it is assumed that during November–March (1) no water evaporates from the wetlands because they are frozen; (2) precipitation, which is less than 20 percent of the annual total (table 3), does not accumulate because it is blown away or evaporates; and (3) runoff does not occur. This last assumption is clearly not always true. In some years, the snowpack in the Benton Lake basin can be large and produce considerable runoff, typically in March when the weather first warms. For example, total runoff (gaging station and ungaged drainages) in late winter of March 1993 and March 2007 was estimated to be 1,600 and 553 acre-ft, respectively (table 6).

Table 8.   Historical mean monthly pan-evaporation data recorded at Benton Lake National Wildlife Refuge and four National Oceanic and Atmospheric Administration weather stations near Benton Lake, Montana, 1916–2008.

[Evaporation data in inches. Data source: 1, Farnsworth and Thompson (1982); 2, National Oceanic and Atmospheric Administration (2009); 3, unpublished water-use reports from Benton Lake National Wildlife Refuge (issued annually). Symbol: --, no data]

| Period | Mean monthly pan-evaporation | | | | | | | Total of mean monthly Apr.–Sept. | Data source |
	Apr.	May	June	July	Aug.	Sept.	Oct.		
Fort Assinniboine									
1948–79	5.05	7.27	7.95	9.94	9.17	5.58	--	44.96	1
1966–2008	4.50	5.66	6.51	8.16	7.19	4.50	--	36.51	2
Moccasin Experiment Station									
1948–79	5.00	6.97	7.79	10.44	9.95	6.51	--	46.66	1
1966–2008	5.07	7.13	7.83	10.49	9.93	6.67	--	47.11	2
Tiber Dam									
1953–75	5.00	6.46	7.02	8.63	7.99	4.78	4.00	39.88	1
1966–75	5.17	5.54	6.42	8.12	7.58	4.69	--	37.51	2
Valier									
1916–78	--	6.79	7.05	8.48	7.87	6.47	3.47	36.66	1
1967–78	5.70	6.54	7.66	6.58	4.72	5.67	--	36.86	2
Benton Lake National Wildlife Refuge Headquarters									
1976–77, 1979–81	3.94	6.10	7.14	8.44	7.90	3.95	3.37	37.47	3

Digital Model for Planning Water Management at Benton Lake National Wildlife Refuge

Description of the Digital Model

The digital model developed for planning water management at Benton Lake NWR uses a water-accounting spreadsheet that tracks inputs and outputs to each of the wetland units of Benton Lake. The program is based on monthly data because this time step is useful for refuge managers to consider for normal refuge operation and because much of the historical data on wetland water levels are available at this time scale. The model accounts for precipitation, evaporation, and allocation of pumped water and runoff to each wetland unit on a monthly basis for the period from April through October. Initial conditions are input to the model as volume or surface area of water in each wetland unit. The model can be run for a historical or future period of 1–5 years. Precipitation data

and the pan-evaporation coefficient can be input by the user or selected from data provided in the model.

The model contains historical values of the combined means of monthly precipitation for the three NOAA weather stations (table 3) and monthly pan-evaporation data for the Fort Assinniboine weather station (table 9). In addition, the model contains the precipitation-runoff relation used to estimate runoff entering the wetlands (fig. 3) as well as stage-capacity data used to convert water-level data to water volume and flooded surface area for each wetland unit.

During each time step for each wetland unit, the volume of water contributed by precipitation, pumpage, and runoff is added to the initial volume, and the volume lost to evaporation is subtracted. Each of these additions or subtractions is simulated as if it occurs at the beginning of the month. The volume of water added by precipitation is calculated as the product of the monthly precipitation rate and the flooded area, which is determined from the sum of the beginning water volume and water volume added by any inflows of pumped water and runoff. Similarly, water lost by evaporation is calculated as the product of the monthly evaporation rate and the flooded area,

Table 9. Monthly pan-evaporation data recorded at the weather station at Fort Assinniboine, Montana, 1966–2008.

[Evaporation data in inches. For years with no data for a specific month, total calculated using the mean monthly value for that month. Data from National Oceanic and Atmospheric Administration (2009). Symbol: --, no data]

Year	Apr.	May	June	July	Aug.	Sept.	Total
1966	--	--	--	9.46	7.41	6.01	39.55
1967	--	5.24	5.74	9.41	8.42	5.42	38.73
1968	4.91	5.58	5.51	8.55	6.32	2.82	33.69
1969	4.50	5.70	5.60	8.07	9.15	5.38	38.40
1970	5.35	--	6.80	7.15	7.37	3.59	35.92
1971	3.38	6.38	6.55	8.53	8.99	4.46	38.29
1972	5.01	5.14	8.00	6.87	7.59	4.16	36.77
1973	4.28	6.53	6.30	8.94	7.72	4.02	37.79
1974	3.54	3.96	7.74	9.45	5.80	3.67	34.16
1975	--	4.78	5.82	8.18	5.81	4.07	33.16
1976	4.42	6.82	5.63	8.41	7.60	5.76	38.64
1977	5.86	5.21	7.13	8.21	5.19	3.49	35.09
1978	2.96	4.25	6.30	6.96	6.55	3.86	30.88
1979	--	4.82	7.55	7.65	6.97	4.82	36.31
1980	5.95	7.49	6.33	8.37	5.82	3.84	37.80
1981	4.79	4.77	5.10	7.47	7.24	4.71	34.08
1982	--	4.70	5.44	7.08	6.99	4.64	33.35
1983	4.02	5.82	6.50	7.55	8.08	4.94	36.91
1984	--	8.80	6.63	9.40	8.29	4.09	41.71
1985	4.27	5.98	8.11	9.96	5.30	2.28	35.90
1986	--	5.01	7.33	6.76	6.52	2.21	32.33
1987	--	5.30	7.73	6.98	5.60	4.39	34.50
1988	5.87	8.13	8.68	9.85	8.47	5.01	46.01
1989	3.50	4.59	5.91	8.39	6.53	3.49	32.41
1990	4.07	4.36	7.22	8.22	8.10	6.34	38.31
1991	4.24	4.93	6.16	8.34	8.02	5.06	36.75
1992	4.99	6.98	7.09	5.85	6.18	4.20	35.29
1993	3.53	5.26	5.84	4.81	5.11	4.35	28.90
1994	4.84	5.86	6.92	9.18	7.48	5.97	40.25
1995	3.38	4.98	6.10	6.02	5.74	3.43	29.65
1996	4.13	3.71	6.86	8.24	8.41	4.67	36.02
1997	--	5.95	6.87	7.73	7.71	5.57	38.33
1998	4.51	7.00	6.34	8.17	8.22	5.72	39.96
1999	--	5.16	6.54	7.03	5.66	4.28	33.17
2000	4.96	6.09	3.95	--	--	5.17	35.51
2001	--	6.76	6.82	8.36	8.20	5.36	40.00
2002	--	5.66	--	8.22	5.04	4.12	34.05
2003	4.54	5.60	6.13	10.24	8.92	4.33	39.76

Table 9. Monthly pan-evaporation data recorded at the weather station at Fort Assinniboine, Montana, 1966–2008.—Continued

[Evaporation data in inches. For years with no data for a specific month, total calculated using the mean monthly value for that month. Data from National Oceanic and Atmospheric Administration (2009). Symbol: --, no data]

Year	Apr.	May	June	July	Aug.	Sept.	Total
2004	5.54	4.86	5.47	7.03	6.57	4.33	33.80
2005	--	7.36	5.70	8.04	8.09	4.65	38.34
2006	4.34	6.32	7.00	11.12	8.24	5.13	42.15
2007	--	5.16	6.97	9.67	7.87	5.27	39.44
2008	4.81	5.05	6.52	8.64	8.53	4.49	38.04
Mean monthly							
	4.50	5.66	6.51	8.16	7.19	4.50	36.51

Table 10. Monthly pan-evaporation data recorded at the weather stations at Benton Lake and Fort Assinniboine, Montana, 1976–77, 1979–81.

[Data from Benton Lake National Wildlife Refuge (issued annually) and National Oceanic and Atmospheric Administration (2009). Symbol: --, no data]

Year	Monthly pan evaporation (inches)								Annual period of record
	Apr.	May	June	July	Aug.	Sept.	Oct.	Total (Apr.–Sept.)	
Benton Lake National Wildlife Refuge Headquarters									
1976	4.18	7.83	6.68	9.32	8.38	6.43	4.10	42.82	--
1977	6.75	7.31	9.43	10.39	7.05	4.20	1.27	45.13	--
1979	1.10	2.97	10.09	8.65	9.41	2.40	5.70	34.62	4/11/79 to 10/22/79
1980	3.71	7.44	2.90	8.14	6.47	2.10	4.00	30.76	4/16/80 to 10/7/80
1981	--	4.95	6.60	5.70	8.20	4.61	1.80	30.06	4/16/81 to 10/5/81
Mean monthly									
	3.94	6.10	7.14	8.44	7.90	3.95	3.37	37.47	
Fort Assinniboine									
1976	4.42	6.82	5.63	8.41	7.60	5.76	--	38.64	4/2/76 to 9/30/76
1977	5.86	5.21	7.13	8.21	5.19	3.49	--	35.09	4/7/77 to 9/30/77
1979	2.05	4.82	7.55	7.65	6.97	4.82	--	33.86	4/14/79 to 9/30/79
1980	5.95	7.49	6.33	8.37	5.82	3.84	--	37.80	4/4/80 to 9/30/80
1981	4.79	4.77	5.10	7.47	7.24	4.71	--	34.08	4/3/81 to 9/30/81
Mean monthly									
	4.61	5.82	6.35	8.02	6.56	4.52	--	35.89	

which is determined from the sum of the beginning water volume and water volume added by precipitation and any inflows.

Calibration of the Digital Model

The model was calibrated by matching historical monthly water-volume data. Calibration of the model was conducted for 1991–95, 1998–99, and 2004–08. Data for years prior to 1991, the first full year of operation of the gaging station on Lake Creek, were not used for calibration because of the greater uncertainty in the data for pumped-water and runoff volumes, which were estimated from water-level data. The 1991–95 period was selected because it encompassed a range of wet and dry years and because the volumes of pumped water and runoff were generally greater than in later years (table 6). The 2004–08 period was selected because it was familiar to current (2009) refuge staff and because the volumes of pumped water and runoff were generally smaller than in earlier years. The 1998–99 period was selected to provide additional calibration data. For each of these 12 calibration years, historical data for monthly amounts of precipitation (table 3), evaporation (table 9), inflows of pumped water and runoff as measured at the Lake Creek gaging station (table 6), and ungaged runoff from other drainages estimated from measured changes in water levels in wetland units before and after precipitation events (table 6) were used as model input. Starting conditions were water volumes measured on April 1 of the calibration year.

Volumes of water transferred between units in monthly time steps were input to match measured monthly water-volume data as closely as possible for each unit. November was included in the model calibration for 1995, 1998, 1999, and 2005 because a substantial amount of pumped water (33–607 acre-ft) entered Benton Lake during November of these years; precipitation and evaporation for November were assumed to be zero.

Although monthly water levels measured in each unit were used as calibration data, these data are not always representative of the water level throughout a wetland unit. For example, measurements made during periods of high wind may not be representative of unit-wide water levels because water levels can be higher at the downwind end of a unit. Also, in some units, the staff gages used to measure water levels are located near the inlet where water is transferred from the interunit canal to the unit, and therefore, the measured water level can reflect the higher level of the water flowing from the canal (Robert F. Johnson, Jr., Benton Lake NWR, oral commun., 2009). Therefore, simulated water levels for Units 3–6 typically were less than the measured values for months when water was flowing into the unit when water levels were recorded.

The success of the model calibration was determined using a calculated value called the "net change in water volume." This value represents the sum of the simulated amounts of water that had to be added to or subtracted from each wetland unit to match measured monthly water-volume data as closely as possible. For each unit, inflows were assigned positive values and outflows were assigned negative values. Water added by precipitation, pumping from Muddy Creek, and runoff, as well as water lost to evaporation, were not included in this calculation. The net change in water volume for all units was calculated for each month, and the monthly values for the entire calibration year were summed to calculate the total net change in water volume. A net change in water volume equal to zero indicated that all simulated transfers of water among the units balanced out. A positive net change in water volume resulted when additional water needed to be added to increase the simulated water volumes in a unit to match the measured values. A positive net change in water volume indicated that either the evaporation rates used in the model were too high or the hydrologic inputs, such as precipitation or runoff, were too low. A negative net change in water volume resulted when water needed to be removed to decrease simulated water volumes in a unit to match the measured values. A negative net change in water volume indicated that either the evaporation rates were too low or the hydrologic inputs were too high.

A large unknown for each calibration year was the actual timing and quantity of water transferred from Unit 1 to Unit 2 and then from Unit 2 to Units 3–6. Specific information on when or how much water was transferred from one unit to another is not available. The only data that document these transfers are the water-level measurements reported in the annual water-use reports (Benton Lake National Wildlife Refuge, issued annually). Therefore, calibration of the model involved adjusting the timing and quantity of transfers of water to individual units so that simulated water levels matched measured water levels and the total net change in water volume was as close to zero as possible.

Model Calibration Using Measured Pan-Evaporation Data

For the first round of model calibration, pan-evaporation data measured at the Fort Assinniboine weather station (table 9) were used for each calibration year. If a monthly value for a specific year was missing, the mean value for that month during 1966–2008 was used. The pan-evaporation coefficient was 0.73, as indicated in Farnsworth and others (1982) for the Benton Lake area. The total net change in water volume for the 12 calibration years ranged widely from +980 acre-ft to -1,950 acre-ft (table 11).

The annual variability in the pan-evaporation data appears to be the cause of the wide range in total net change in water volumes for several reasons. First, the total net change in water volume for a calibration year appears to be positively correlated to the April–September measured pan evaporation at Fort Assinniboine for that calibration year (fig. 4A). In years when pan evaporation was low (less than about 37 in.), the total net change in water volume was negative and large. Conversely, in years when pan evaporation was high (greater than

Table 11. Summary of data output for model calibration using measured pan-evaporation data from Fort Assinniboine, Montana, and a pan-evaporation coefficient of 0.73.

[Runoff includes runoff conveyed through Lake Creek to Benton Lake and diffuse runoff from other channels to Benton Lake. Total water volume on October 31 shown for 1995, 1998, 1999, and 2005 is for November 30]

Year	Hydrologic inputs and output (acre-feet)					Net change in water volume (acre-feet)									Total simulated water volume (acre-feet)	
	Precipi-tation	Pumped water	Runoff	Total inputs	Evapor-ation	Apr.	May	June	July	Aug.	Sept.	Oct.	Nov.	Total	Apr. 1	Oct. 31
1991	3,466	7,043	991	11,500	-8,928	140	10	-780	0	10	-270	-40	0	-930	1,486	3,128
1992	3,249	6,574	9	9,832	-8,160	210	340	100	-65	-250	-900	-175	0	-740	1,843	2,775
1993	6,560	1,718	1,425	9,703	-8,611	-170	-40	-190	-520	-680	-550	200	0	-1,950	4,474	3,616
1994	2,717	5,611	54	8,382	-9,216	220	-20	-220	-100	-50	-110	180	0	-100	3,275	2,341
1995	3,527	5,559	390	9,476	-7,601	70	200	180	-60	-170	-760	-150	-150	-840	1,583	2,618
1998	4,159	5,693	736	10,588	-10,434	-30	590	-40	0	-30	480	0	-260	710	2,702	3,566
1999	3,103	5,033	122	8,258	-7,558	-365	400	-170	0	0	-210	-70	-230	-645	3,028	3,083
2004	2,473	3,985	73	6,531	-5,207	10	280	5	-60	-40	-480	-265	0	-550	1,616	2,390
2005	2,289	2,849	885	6,023	-6,244	0	20	-175	-50	-60	345	360	-100	340	2,049	2,168
2006	3,859	3,951	2,419	10,229	-9,657	-75	-50	-405	0	100	470	370	0	410	1,891	2,873
2007	2,342	3,542	54	5,938	-7,157	-25	-30	0	0	210	-25	130	0	260	2,727	1,768
2008	3,152	4,204	837	8,193	-7,738	35	480	390	20	-230	-65	350	0	980	1,347	2,782
Mean	3,408	4,647	666	8,721	-8,043	2	182	-109	-70	-99	-173	74	-60	-255	2,335	2,759

about 38 in.), the total net change in water volume typically was positive. Second, the simulated decrease in water volumes in individual units was less than the measured decreases during summer months with low pan evaporation. This phenomenon is shown well in 1995, when simulated water volumes in Units 3, 4C, 5, and 6 were greater than measured volumes during much of July, August, and September (fig. 5). Finally, total net change in water volume was not well correlated to other hydrologic factors, such as the amount of runoff, pumped water, or precipitation, which points to the measured pan-evaporation data as not being representative of actual conditions at Benton Lake.

The wide range in total net change in water volume for the 12 calibration years demonstrates that using the measured pan-evaporation data does not produce representative results. In addition, the distribution of the results in relation to pan evaporation (fig. 4A) has a systematic pattern of insufficient water loss for years with low pan evaporation (negative total net change in water volume) and excess water loss for years with high pan evaporation (positive total net change in water volume). This pattern suggests that using the same evaporation rates for all years might provide a better match to measured water volumes for all calibration years.

Model Calibration Using Mean Monthly Pan-Evaporation Data

For the second round of model calibration, the same evaporation data were used for each calibration year. These data were the mean monthly values of pan evaporation for the Fort Assinniboine weather station for 1966–2008 (table 9). During calibration, the pan-evaporation coefficient was varied

until most of the total net change in water volume values were near zero. This final pan-evaporation coefficient was 0.77, which is about 5 percent higher than the 0.73 value indicated by Farnsworth and others (1982) for the Benton Lake area. This higher pan-evaporation coefficient appears to be reasonable because May–October pan evaporation in the Benton Lake area (about 45 in.), as indicated in Farnsworth and others (1982), is about 5 percent higher than in the Fort Assinniboine area (about 43 in.). Similarly, on the basis of comparison of the short term record at refuge headquarters with Fort Assinniboine (table 10), pan evaporation at Benton Lake is about 4 percent higher than at Fort Assinniboine.

An example of simulated results for a single calibration year is shown in figure 6 and table 12 for 1995. These results are illustrative of several features of the model-calibration effort. First, although water-volume data may be available for dates within any given month, only beginning-of-month measured values are used for calibration. Second, measured water levels in Units 3–6 can be artificially high, primarily owing to the proximity of staff gages to inflowing water. Therefore, simulated water-volume values typically are less than measured values during periods when water was flowing into a unit. This discrepancy is apparent for Units 3 and 4C on June 1 (fig. 6). Third, evaporation in Units 3–6 appears to be simulated well during July and August when little if any water was being transferred (table 12) because simulated water volumes decrease at about the same rate from month to month as the measured values.

The total net change in water volume for the 12 calibration years ranged from +1,035 acre-ft to -505 acre-ft (table 13), and the mean for these 12 years (+134 acre-ft) was close to zero. In addition, the values of total net change in water volume for individual years were distributed fairly

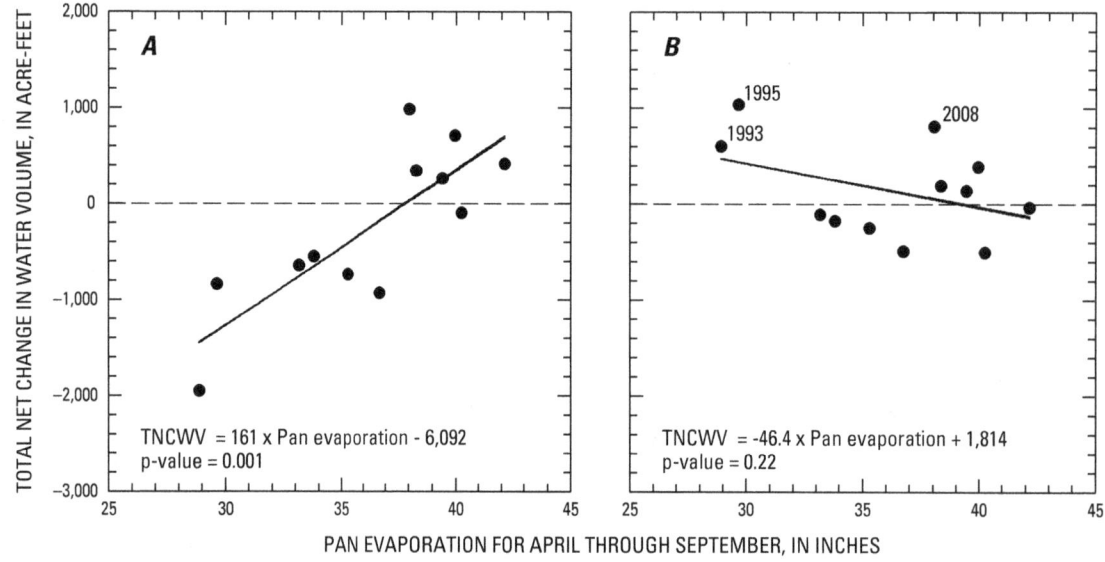

Figure 4.　Relation of April–September pan evaporation measured at Fort Assinniboine, Montana, to total net change in water volume (TNCWV) for simulated results produced using A, measured and B, mean monthly pan-evaporation data.

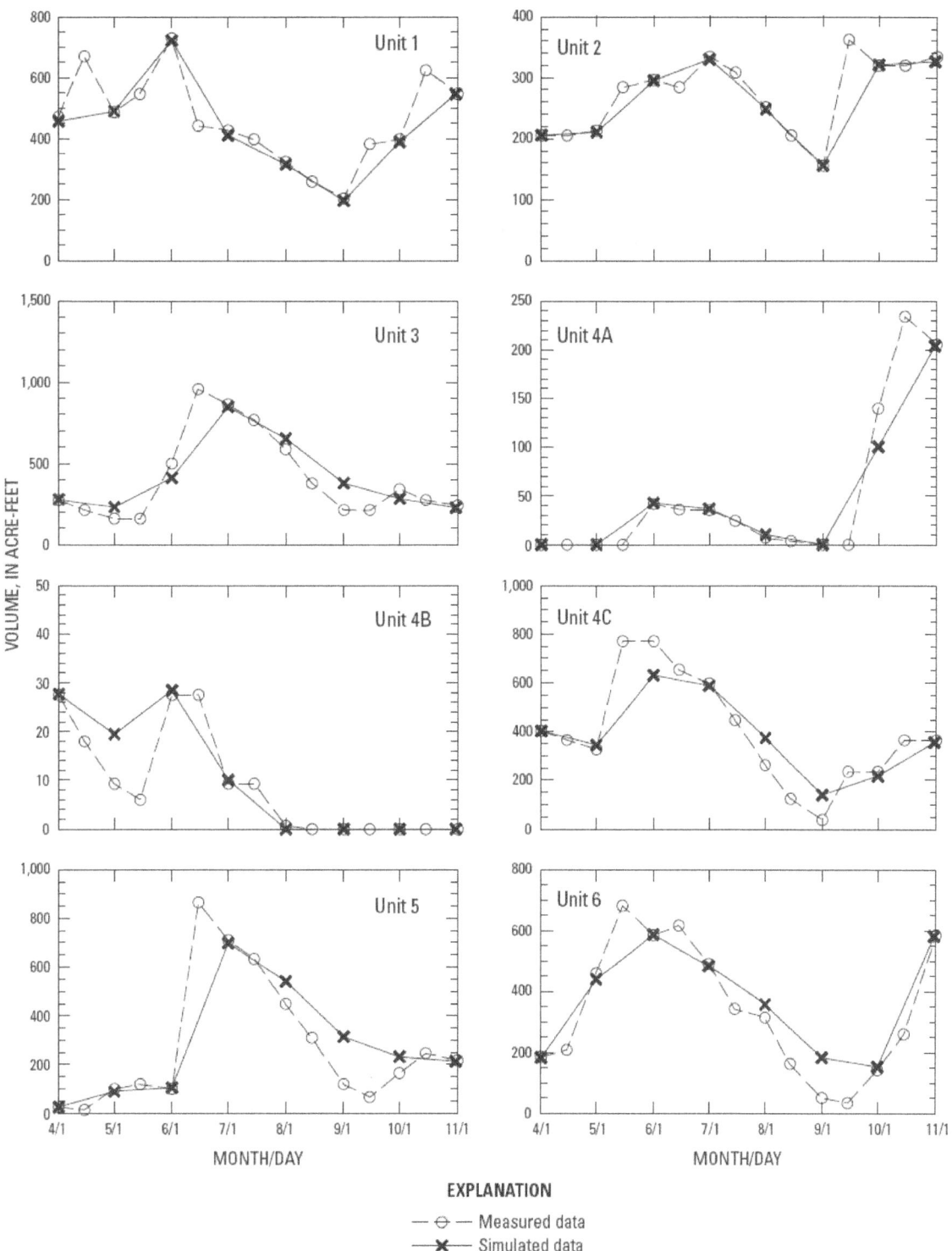

Figure 5.   Comparison of measured and simulated water volumes for 1995 using measured pan-evaporation data from Fort Assinniboine, Montana, and a pan-evaporation coefficient of 0.73.

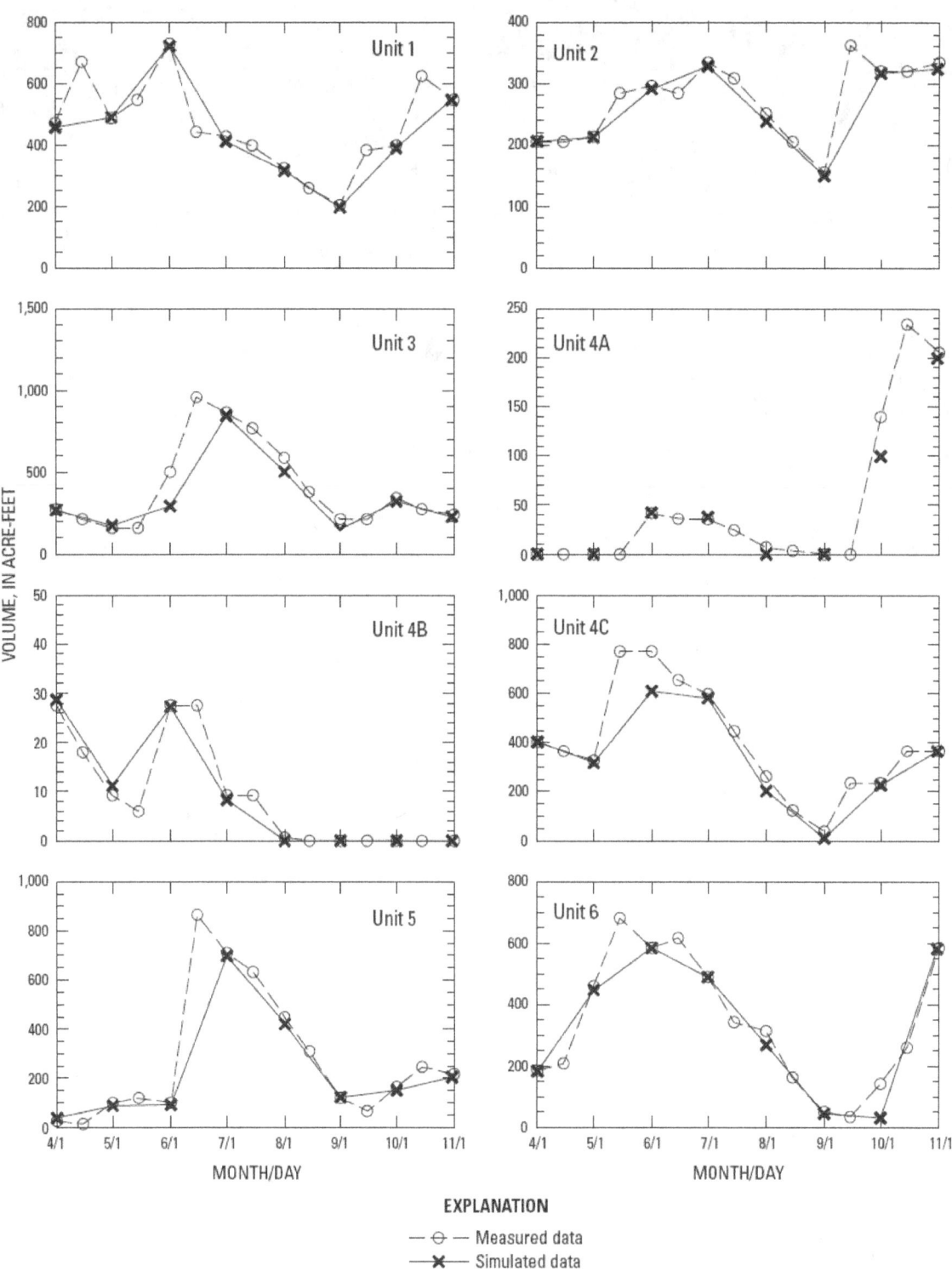

Figure 6.   Comparison of measured and simulated water volumes for 1995 using mean monthly pan-evaporation data for 1966–2008 from Fort Assinniboine, Montana, and a pan-evaporation coefficient of 0.77.

evenly with respect to the April–September pan evaporation measured at Fort Assinniboine for the calibration years (fig. 4B). This even distribution is supported by the slope of the regression line, which is not significantly different from zero based on the p-value of 0.22. (fig. 4B). A p-value less than 0.05 would indicate that the slope of the regression line was significantly different than zero (Helsel and Hirsch, 2002). Overall, the model calibrated with mean monthly pan-evaporation data is considered to be more representative of actual conditions at Benton Lake than the model calibrated with measured pan-evaporation data.

The results for the calibration of the model using mean monthly pan evaporation are better than for the model using measured pan evaporation for several reasons. First, the mean total net change in water volume was closer to zero (+134 acre-ft for mean monthly evaporation and -255 acre-ft for measured evaporation). Second, the distribution of values of total net change in water volume was more even in relation to measured pan-evaporation as shown by the slope of the regressions in figure 4. The slope was not significantly different from zero (p-value greater than 0.05) for mean monthly evaporation but significantly different from zero (p-value less than 0.05) for measured evaporation. Finally, the range of the values of total net change in water volume was

smaller for mean monthly evaporation (+1,035 to -505 acre-ft) than for measured evaporation (+980 to -1,950 acre-ft). For each calibration year, the total net change in water volume produced with the model using mean monthly evaporation represents less than 11 percent of the total inflow (precipitation, pumped water, and runoff), which ranged from about 5,800 to 11,500 acre-ft among all calibration years. This level of uncertainty is considered acceptable by water managers at Benton Lake NWR, and thus the model provides a useful tool for planning at the refuge.

Limitations

Although the digital model for planning water management at Benton Lake simulates as many as 5 consecutive years, the exclusion of the winter periods (November–March) can be a potential problem. In general, water volume tends to decrease during the winter as water lost to evaporation (and sublimation when Benton Lake is frozen) typically exceeds any water gained from precipitation and snowmelt runoff. This change in water volume during the winter is shown in the right-hand column of table 13. This change in water volume during the winter period typically is between about -100 and -700 acre-ft, and the mean is -253 acre-ft (table 13). The large

Table 12. Summary of simulated inflows, outflows, water transfers, and flooded surface area for model calibration for 1995 using mean monthly pan-evaporation data for 1966–2008 from Fort Assinniboine, Montana, and a pan-evaporation coefficient of 0.77.

[Symbol: --, no data]

Inflow, outflow, water transfers, or flooded surface area	Apr.	May	June	July	Aug.	Sept.	Oct.	Nov.	Year
Inflows and outflows to and from Benton Lake (acre-feet)									
Precipitation	420	838	941	642	128	281	302	0	3,552
Inflow to Unit 1 from Lake Creek	380	1,180	1,070	3	77	1,490	1,370	324	5,894
Diffuse runoff	0	33	22	0	0	0	0	0	55
Evaporation	-903	-1,471	-1,874	-2,111	-1,377	-954	-814	0	-9,504
Water transfers between units (acre-feet)									
Unit 1	-300	-893	-1,320	0	-100	-1,240	-1,170	-250	-5,273
Unit 2	40	120	100	10	0	225	45	90	630
Unit 3	0	240	720	0	0	340	0	0	1,300
Unit 4A	0	70	10	0	0	150	140	0	370
Unit 4B	0	38	0	0	0	0	0	0	38
Unit 4C	40	480	220	0	0	370	270	0	1,380
Unit 5	120	80	770	0	0	150	140	0	1,260
Unit 6	360	240	40	0	0	50	640	0	1,330
Total net change in water volume (Unit 1 through Unit 6; acre-feet)									
	260	375	540	10	-100	45	65	-160	1,035
Flooded surface area at end of month (acres)									
Benton Lake	2,724	2,643	3,557	4,047	2,997	1,418	2,489	3,341	--

Table 13. Summary of data ouput for model calibration using mean monthly pan-evaporation data for 1966–2008 from Fort Assinniboine, Montana, and a pan-evaporation coefficient of 0.77.

[Runoff includes runoff conveyed through Lake Creek to Benton Lake and diffuse runoff from other channels to Benton Lake. Total water volume on October 31 shown for 1995, 1998, 1999, and 2005 is for November 30. Symbol: --, no data]

Year	Hydrologic inputs and output (acre-feet)					Net change in water volume (acre-feet)									Total simulated water volume (acre-feet)		
	Precipi-tation	Pumped water	Runoff	Total inputs	Evapor-ation	Apr.	May	June	July	Aug.	Sept.	Oct.	Nov.	Total	Apr. 1	Oct. 31	Change during previous winter
1991	3,480	7,043	991	11,514	-9,359	195	210	-565	0	70	-300	-105	0	-495	1,486	3,146	--
1992	3,186	6,574	9	9,762	-8,594	190	25	30	20	-140	-295	-85	0	-255	1,843	2,763	-1,303
1993	6,552	1,718	1,425	9,695	-11,176	75	-30	-150	200	175	120	210	0	600	4,474	3,593	1,711
1994	2,708	5,611	54	8,373	-8,820	155	30	-220	-130	-120	-410	190	0	-505	3,275	2,323	-318
1995	3,552	5,559	390	9,499	-9,504	260	375	540	10	-100	45	65	-160	1,035	1,583	2,615	-741
1998	4,089	5,693	736	10,518	-9,941	-100	260	170	0	-40	135	10	-50	385	2,702	3,664	--
1999	3,141	5,033	122	8,296	-8,040	-175	470	-130	0	0	-170	150	-260	-115	3,028	3,169	-631
2004	2,582	3,985	73	6,641	-5,767	0	350	20	0	70	-405	-165	0	-130	1,616	2,360	--
2005	2,364	2,849	885	6,097	-6,291	0	-40	-155	-40	-90	220	390	-100	185	2,049	2,041	-311
2006	3,883	3,951	2,419	10,253	-9,235	-60	-80	-415	-90	-10	225	390	0	-40	1,891	2,869	-128
2007	2,253	3,542	54	5,849	-6,952	15	0	0	-50	96	-36	110	0	135	2,727	1,759	-142
2008	3,120	4,204	837	8,160	-7,527	30	360	380	-30	-70	-35	170	0	805	1,347	2,786	-412
Mean	3,409	4,647	666	8,721	-8,434	49	161	-41	-9	-13	-76	111	-48	134	2,335	2,763	-253

decrease (-1,303 acre-ft; table 13) during winter 1991–92 is atypical and difficult to explain. A possible explanation is that the wetland units lost their winter ice cover in February, a month earlier than usual (Benton Lake National Wildlife Refuge, issued annually), and thus allowed evaporation to occur for a longer period than usual during the late winter. For all the calibration years, total water volume in winter increased substantially only once. Between the end of October 1992 and the beginning of April 1993, the total water volume increased by 1,711 acre-ft (table 13). Much of this increase (1,600 acre-ft; table 6) resulted from melting during March of the unusually large winter snowpack that had accumulated in the Benton Lake basin.

The accuracy of the water-level/capacity data for the wetland units is not known. These data are based on topographic surveys conducted in the 1960s. Any subsequent natural or anthropogenic modifications to individual units are not reflected in these data. Possible modifications include deflation, siltation, changes in vegetation, and earth-moving projects.

As noted in the "Hydrologic Inputs" section, estimation of runoff is based on a relation between monthly precipitation and monthly runoff, and therefore is imprecise. In addition, the model does not automatically incorporate atypical runoff events, such as runoff from a large winter snowpack (as occurred in 1978) or exceptionally cold and rainy periods (such as 1993). However, different or atypical runoff can be simulated in the program by manually adding water for winter carryover or for specific months.

As noted in the "Hydrologic Outputs" section, an additional loss of wetland water could occur when a dry wetland unit is flooded and some of the inflowing water is lost to resaturation of the desiccated bottom sediment. This resaturation loss is assumed to be zero in the model because no data are available to quantify this potential type of water loss.

Summary and Conclusions

Benton Lake National Wildlife Refuge (NWR) is an important area for waterfowl production and migratory stopover in west-central Montana. Eight wetland units covering about 5,600 acres are the essential features of the refuge. Water availability in the wetland units can be uncertain owing to the large natural variations in precipitation and runoff. The U.S. Geological Survey, in cooperation with the U.S. Fish and Wildlife Service, has developed a digital model for planning water management. The model can simulate strategies for water transfers among the wetland units and account for variability in runoff and pumped water.

The model is based on a conceptual model of the hydrologic system of Benton Lake. Water entering Benton Lake comes from precipitation, pumpage from Muddy Creek, and runoff. Water is lost from Benton Lake by evaporation. Water can be moved by gravity flow between the wetland units. In

general, water stored in the lake has no net long-term gain or loss.

The digital model developed for planning water management at Benton Lake NWR uses a water-accounting spreadsheet. The program accounts for inputs, outputs, and transfers of water between wetland units on a monthly basis for the period from April through October. Initial conditions are input to the model as volume or surface area of water in each wetland unit. The program can be run for a historical or future period of 1–5 years. Input to the model includes (1) monthly values for precipitation, water pumped from Muddy Creek, runoff, and evaporation; (2) water-level/capacity data for each wetland unit; and (3) the pan-evaporation coefficient. Output includes monthly water volume and flooded surface area for each unit for as many as 5 consecutive years.

The water-management model was calibrated by comparing simulated and historical measured water volumes for 1991–95, 1998–99, and 2004–08. Using measured pan-evaporation data did not produce representative results; thus it was believed that using the same evaporation rates for all years might provide a better match to measured water volumes for all calibration years. Computed on the basis of mean monthly evaporation data, the mean total net change in water volume was about +134 acre-ft, which indicates the water-balance discrepancies were, on average, close to zero. The total net change in water volume for these 12 years ranged from +1,035 to -505 acre-ft. These values represent less than 11 percent of the total annual inflow. This level of uncertainty is considered acceptable by water managers at Benton Lake NWR, and thus the model provides a useful tool for planning at the refuge.

Limitations of the model include the exclusion of the winter periods (November–March), the accuracy of the water-level/capacity data, and the difficulty in estimating runoff and predicting atypical runoff events. In addition, the model does not account for water lost to resaturation of dry wetland sediment when units are flooded.

References

Benton Lake National Wildlife Refuge, issued annually, Water use report, Benton Lake National Wildlife Refuge: Great Falls, Montana [unpublished reports for 1964–2008, variously paged].

Dunne, Thomas, and Leopold, L.B., 1978, Water in environmental planning: San Francisco, W.H. Freeman and Company, 818 p.

Farnsworth, R.K., and Thompson, E.S., 1982, Mean monthly, seasonal, and annual pan evaporation for the United States: National Oceanic and Atmospheric Administration Technical Report NWS 34, 82 p.

Farnsworth, R.K., Thompson, E.S., and Peck, E.L., 1982, Evaporation atlas for the contiguous 48 United States: National Oceanic and Atmospheric Administration Technical Report NWS 33, 26 p.

Helsel, D.R., and Hirsch, R.M., 2002, Statistical methods in water resources: U.S. Geological Survey Techniques of Water Resources Investigations, book 4, chap. A3, 522 p.

National Oceanic and Atmospheric Administration, 2009, Locate weather observation station record: National Oceanic and Atmospheric Administration database, accessed March 3, 2009, at *http://www.ncdc.noaa.gov/oa/climate/ stationlocator.html*.

Nimick, D.A., 1997, Hydrology and water chemistry of the Benton Lake basin with emphasis on the fate of dissolved solids at Benton Lake National Wildlife Refuge, west-central Montana: U.S. Geological Survey Water-Resources Investigations Report 97–4100, 79 p.

Nimick, D.A., Lambing, J.H., Palawski, D.U., and Malloy, J.C., 1996, Detailed study of selenium in soil, water, bottom sediment, and biota in the Sun River Irrigation Project, Freezout Lake Wildlife Management Area, and Benton Lake National Wildlife Refuge, west-central Montana, 1990–92: U.S. Geological Survey Water-Resources Investigations Report 95–4170, 120 p.

Omang, R.J., and Parrett, Charles, 1984, A method for estimating mean annual runoff of ungaged streams based on basin characteristics in central and eastern Montana: U.S. Geological Survey Water-Resources Investigations Report 84–4143, 15 p.

Appendixes

The instructions for using the model are in appendix 1. The digital model, which is compiled and organized into a Microsoft Excel file that contains eight worksheets, is in appendix 2. Appendix 2 is located in the CD–ROM on the inside back cover of this report or is available at *http://pubs.usgs.gov/sir/2011/5133*.

Appendix 1: Instructions for Using the Digital Model for Planning Water Management at Benton Lake National Wildlife Refuge

A model was developed to aid in planning water management for the eight wetland units at Benton Lake National Wildlife Refuge. The model was developed using Microsoft Visual Basic (VBA) and runs in Microsoft Excel 2007. To run the model, the user will have to (1) ensure that macros are enabled in Excel, (2) click the "Office" button in the upper left corner of the window, and (3) navigate to Excel Options>Trust Center>Trust Center Settings>Macro Settings and then select "Trust access to the VBA project object model." The main Excel file contains the VB code and eight worksheets: "Start," "Final Output," "Calculation Sheet," "Area.Volume Tables," "Runoff," "Precipitation," "Previous Data," and "Help." Tabs for these worksheets are located at the bottom of the Excel window. Users are warned that the worksheets have additional data that are essential to the model computations and must not be changed or deleted. To help ensure that users do not inadvertently change important data, some worksheets are protected with the password "flood." The "Help" worksheet contains additional information about using the model.

From the "Start" worksheet, the user can either start the model or manage saved data. Selecting the "Manage Saved Data" option brings up another dialogue box in which saved datasets can be deleted. Selecting the "Program" option brings up the first dialog box for entering data for a simulation. At this point, a saved dataset can be selected, or a new simulation can be started by filling in the requested starting-conditions information. Initial water volumes in each unit, the time period to be simulated, the method for determining precipitation, and the pan-evaporation coefficient are entered in this dialogue box. Historical precipitation data for 1991–2008 and statistically determined precipitation data for dry, average, wet, and very wet years are available within the model. A default value of 0.77 is used for the pan-evaporation coefficient, but any value between 0.5 and 1.0 can be entered instead. Selecting the "Finished" option brings up the second dialogue box for entering data for the simulation.

The second dialogue box for data entry is used to indicate the monthly volume of runoff and pumped water entering each of the eight wetland units. In reality, pumped water and runoff from Lake Creek enter Unit 1 and then are transferred immediately or at a later time to the other wetland units by gravity flow through headgates and the interunit canal. In the model, inflows and transfers of these inflows are assumed to occur in the same month; thus, the water-volume data entered for each wetland unit into the dialogue box represents the net result of inflows and transfers.

The second dialogue box has a separate input array for each year of the simulation. The volumes of water are summarized in the lower half and the right-hand side of the dialogue box. The lower half of the dialogue box also shows how much runoff enters Benton Lake each month. Any amount of water that exceeds the volume of runoff is considered to have been pumped to the refuge, although in reality, this extra water could be considered additional runoff if desired by the user. Negative numbers can be entered to remove water from a unit. For the second through fifth years, the net volume of water that is lost or gained during the previous winter can be entered; the default carryover volume is -200 acre-ft or less if less than 200 acre-ft water is available to be lost. The second dialogue box opens on the "Calculation Sheet" worksheet next to eight graphs showing total volume and surface area for each unit for April through October for the simulation year selected in the dialogue box. The total monthly volumes displayed on the graphs for each unit reflect not only the volumes of runoff and pumped water for each month being input by the user, but also the volumes of precipitation and evaporation occurring each month. The graphs are continually updated while data are being entered to provide instant feedback to the user. However, data entry goes more quickly if the box for turning off continuous updating is checked. Maximum volume and surface area for each wetland unit are shown on the graphs. If continuous updating is turned on and volume data entered in the second dialog box result in the maximum volume for a unit being exceeded, the model displays a warning message. Selecting the "Finished" option brings up a dialogue box allowing the user to save the simulation input data. After completing the save option, the "Final Output" worksheet appears and shows summary output information and graphs for the entire simulation period. If less than 5 years is chosen for simulation, the model still stimulates data for 5 years; the user should ignore this extraneous output.

Publishing support provided by the:
  Denver and Rolla Publishing Service Centers

For more information concerning this publication, contact:
  Director, Montana Water Science Center
  U.S. Geological Survey
  3162 Bozeman Ave.
  Helena, MT 59601
  (406) 457–5900

Or visit the Montana Water Science Center Web site at:
  http://mt.water.usgs.gov/

USGS

Nimick and others—A Digital Model for Planning Water Management at Benton Lake National Wildlife Refuge, West-Central Montana—SIR 2011–5133

ISBN 978-1-4113-3218-8

9 781411 332188